TV Themes
PAST & PRESENT

ISBN 0-7935-8098-6

HAL•LEONARD®
CORPORATION
7777 W. BLUEMOUND RD. P.O. BOX 13819 MILWAUKEE, WI 53213

Visit Hal Leonard Online at
www.halleonard.com

TV Themes PAST & PRESENT

CONTENTS

The Ballad of Davy Crockett

from Walt Disney's DAVY CROCKETT

Words by TOM BLACKBURN
Music by GEORGE BRUNS

1. Born on a moun-tain top in Ten-nes-see, Green-est state in the
2. eigh-teen-thir-teen the Creeks up-rose, addin' redskin arrows to the
3. Off through the woods he's a marchin' a-long, makin' up yarns an' a-

Land of the Free, Raised in the woods so's he knew ev-'ry tree,
coun-try's woes. Now, In-jun fightin' is some-thin' he knows, so he
sing-in' a song, itch-in' fer fightin' an' right-in' a wrong, He's

kilt him a b'ar when he was on-ly three. Da-vy,
should-ers his rifle an' off he goes. Da-vy,
ringy as a b'ar an' twict as strong. Da-vy,

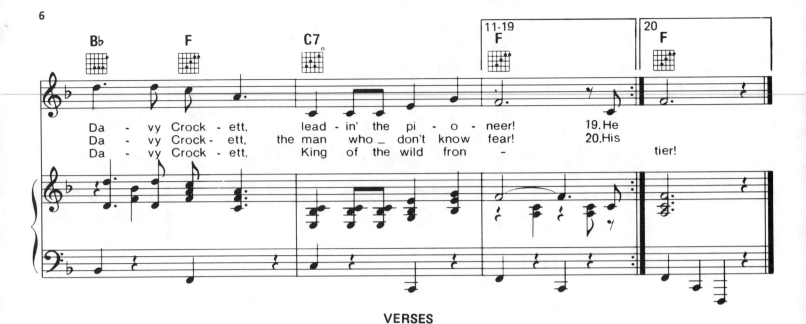

Da - vy Crock - ett, lead - in' the pi - o - neer! 19.He
Da - vy Crock - ett, the man who _ don't know fear! 20.His
Da - vy Crock - ett, King of the wild fron - tier!

VERSES

4.

Andy Jackson is our gen'ral's name,
His reg'lar soldiers we'll put to shame,
Them redskin varmints us Volunteers'll tame,
'Cause we got the guns with the sure-fire aim.
Davy — Davy Crockett,
The champion of us all!

5.

Headed back to war from the ol' home place,
But Red Stick was leadin' a merry chase,
Fightin' an' burnin' at a devil's pace
South to the swamps on the Florida Trace.
Davy — Davy Crockett,
Trackin' the redskins down!

6.

Fought single-handed through the Injun War
Till the Creeks was whipped an' peace was in store,
An' while he was handlin' this risky chore,
Made hisself a legend for evermore.
Davy — Davy Crockett,
King of the wild frontier!

7.

He give his word an' he give his hand
That his Injun friends could keep their land,
An' the rest of his life he took the stand
That justice was due every redskin band.
Davy — Davy Crockett,
Holdin' his promise dear!

8.

Home fer the winter with his family,
Happy as squirrels in the ol' gum tree,
Bein' the father he wanted to be,
Close to his boys as the pod an' the pea.
Davy — Davy Crockett,
Holdin' his young 'uns dear!

9.

But the ice went out an' the warm winds came
An' the meltin' snow showed tracks of game,
An' the flowers of Spring filled the woods with flame,
An' all of a sudden life got too tame.
Davy — Davy Crockett,
Headin' on West again!

10.

Off through the woods we're riding' along,
Makin' up yarns an' singin' a song,
He's ringy as a b'ar an' twict as strong,
An' knows he's right 'cause he ain't often wrong.
Davy — Davy Crockett,
The man who don't know fear!

11.

Lookin' fer a place where the air smells clean,
Where the trees is tall an' the grass is green,
Where the fish is fat in an untouched stream,
An' the teemin' woods is a hunter's dream.
Davy — Davy Crockett,
Lookin' fer Paradise!

12.

Now he'd lost his love an' his grief was gall,
In his heart he wanted to leave it all,
An' lose himself in the forests tall,
But he answered instead his country's call.
Davy — Davy Crockett,
Beginnin' his campaign!

13.

Needin' his help they didn't vote blind,
They put in Davy 'cause he was their kind,
Sent up to Nashville the best they could find,
A fightin' spirit an' a thinkin' mind.
Davy — Davy Crockett,
Choice of the whole frontier!

14.

The votes were counted an' he won hands down,
So they sent him off to Washin'ton town
With his best dress suit still his buckskins brown,
A livin' legend of growin' renown.
Davy — Davy Crockett,
The Canebrake Congressman!

15.

He went off to Congress an' served a spell,
Fixin' up the Gover'ment an' laws as well,
Took over Washin'ton so we heered tell
An' patched up the crack in the Liberty Bell.
Davy — Davy Crockett,
Seein' his duty clear!

16.

Him an' his jokes travelled all through the land,
An' his speeches made him friends to beat the band,
His politickin' was their favorite brand
An' everyone wanted to shake his hand.
Davy — Davy Crockett,
Helpin' his legend grow!

17.

He knew when he spoke he sounded the knell
Of his hopes for White House an' fame as well,
But he spoke out strong so hist'ry books tell
An patched up the crack in the Liberty Bell.
Davy — Davy Crockett,
Seein' his duty clear!

Bandstand Boogie

from the Television Series AMERICAN BANDSTAND

Words by BARRY MANILOW and BRUCE SUSSMAN
Music by CHARLES ALBERTINE

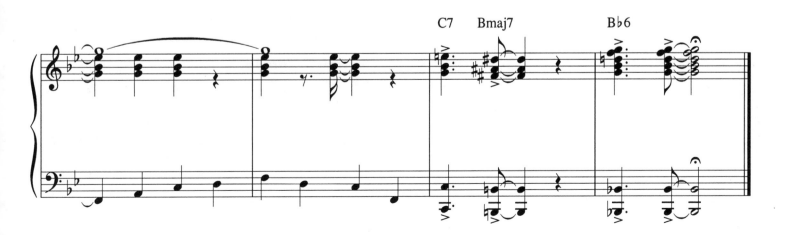

Ballad of Jed Clampett

from the Television Series THE BEVERLY HILLBILLIES

Words and Music by
PAUL HENNING

Not too fast

Come and lis-ten to my sto-ry 'bout a man named Jed,
first thing you know old Jed's a mil-lion-aire,
Jed bought a man-sion, law-dy, it was swank,
now it's time to say good-bye to Jed and all his kin.

poor moun-tain-eer, bare-ly kept his fam-'ly fed. And
kin-folk said, "Jed, move a-way from there." Said,
next door neigh-bor was the pres-'dent of the bank. Lot-sa
They would like to thank you folks for kind-ly drop-pin' in. You're

The Brady Bunch

Theme from the Paramount Television Series THE BRADY BUNCH

Words and Music by SHERWOOD SCHWARTZ
and FRANK DEVOL

Bubbles in the Wine

featured in the Television Series THE LAWRENCE WELK SHOW

Words and Music by FRANK LOESSER,
BOB CALAME and LAWRENCE WELK

Where Everybody Knows Your Name

Theme from the Paramount Television Series CHEERS

Words and Music by GARY PORTNOY
and JUDY HART ANGELO

Mak-ing your way __ in the world __ to-day __ takes ev-'ry-thing __ you got. __
Climb-ing the walls __ when no __ one calls; you've lost at love __ a-gain. __

Tak-ing a break __ from all __ your wor-ries sure would help __ a-lot. __
And the more you're down __ and out, __ the more you need __ a friend, __

Would-n't you like __ to get __ a-way? __ }
when you long to hear a kind __ hel-lo. __ }

Casper the Friendly Ghost
from the Paramount Cartoon

Words by MACK DAVID
Music by JERRY LIVINGSTON

Come On Get Happy

Theme from THE PARTRIDGE FAMILY

Words and Music by WES FARRELL
and DANNY JANSSEN

Hel - lo world__ hear the song ___ that we're sing - in';

come on get hap - py. ___

A

whole lot of lov - in' is what __ we'll be bring - in',

we'll make you hap -

Equalizer - Main Title
from the Television Series

By STEWART COPELAND

Courtship of Eddie's Father

from the Television Series

Words and Music by
HARRY NILSSON

Peo - ple, let me tell you 'bout my best friend; __ he's a warm - heart - ed per - son who'll love __ me till the end. Peo - ple, let me tell you 'bout my best friend; __ he's a one boy, cud - dl - y toy, my up, my down, my pride and joy.

Donna Reed Theme

from the Television Series

By WILLIAM LOOSE
and JOHN SEELY

Father Knows Best Theme

from the Television Series FATHER KNOWS BEST

By DON FERRIS
and IRVING FRIEDMAN

Theme from "Frasier"

from the Paramount Television Series FRASIER

Words by DARRYL PHINNESSEE
Music by BRUCE MILLER

Georgia on My Mind

from the Television Series DESIGNING WOMEN

Words by STUART GORRELL
Music by HOAGY CARMICHAEL

Get Smart
from the Television Series

By IRVING SZATHMARY

Harlem Nocturne
featured in the Television Series MIKE HAMMER

Words by DICK ROGERS
Music by EARLE HAGEN

Hazel

Theme from the Television Production HAZEL

Words and Music by HOWARD GREENFIELD
and JACK KELLER

Hogan's Heroes March

from the Television Series HOGAN'S HEROES

By JERRY FIELDING

58

Home Improvement
Theme from the T.V. Series

Music by DAN FOLIART

The Little House
(On the Prairie)
LITTLE HOUSE ON THE PRAIRIE

Music by DAVID ROSE

Theme from "Magnum, P.I."

from the Universal Television Series MAGNUM, P.I.

By MIKE POST
and PETE CARPENTER

MCA Music Publishing

Major Dad
Theme from the Television Series

By ROGER STEINMAN

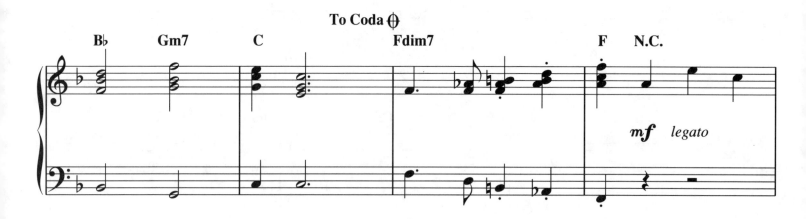

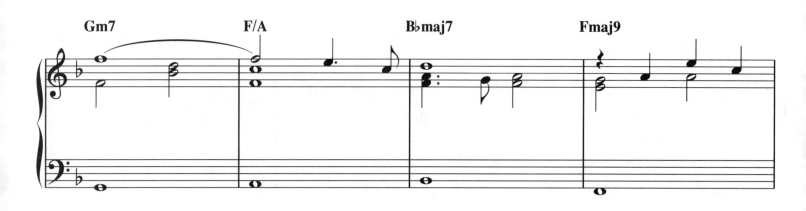

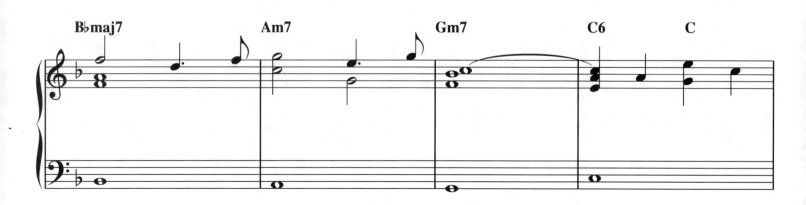

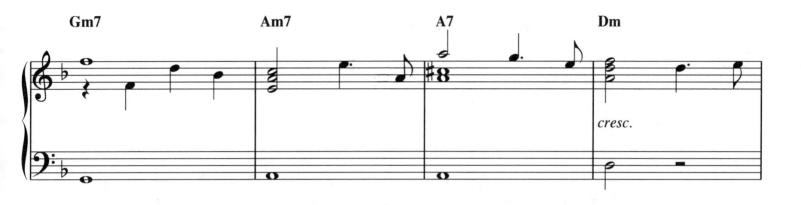

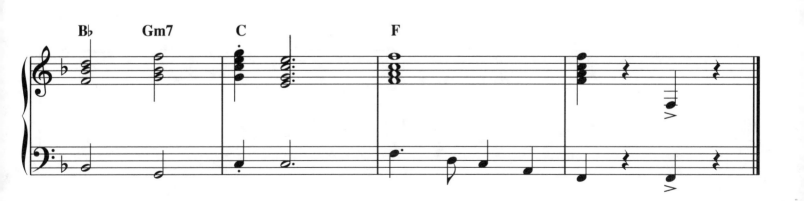

The Masterpiece

the T.V. Theme from MASTERPIECE THEATER

By J.J. MOURET
and PAUL PARNES

Majestically

McHale's Navy March

from the Television Series McHALE'S NAVY

Music by ALEX STORDAHL

The Muppet Show Theme
from the Television Series

By JIM HENSON
and SAM POTTLE

It's time to play the mu - sic. It's time to light the lights.

It's time to meet the Mup - pets on *The Mup - pet Show* to - night.

Mystery
Theme from the PBS Television Series

Music by NORMAND ROGER

Nadia's Theme
from THE YOUNG AND THE RESTLESS

By BARRY DeVORZON
and PERRY BOTKIN, JR.

Theme from "Route 66"

from the Television Series

By NELSON RIDDLE

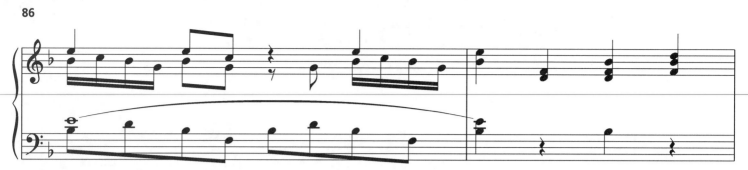

Perry Mason Theme

from the Television Series

By FRED STEINER

Slow and dramatic

A tempo ♩= 88

Bass well marked (con 8va-ad lib.)

Quincy

Theme from the Universal Television Series QUINCY

Words and Music by GLEN LARSON
and STU PHILLIPS

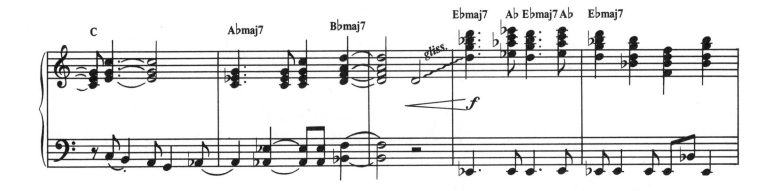

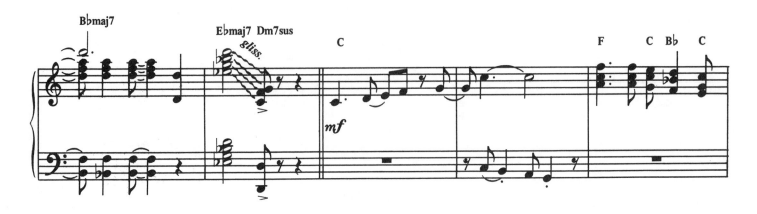

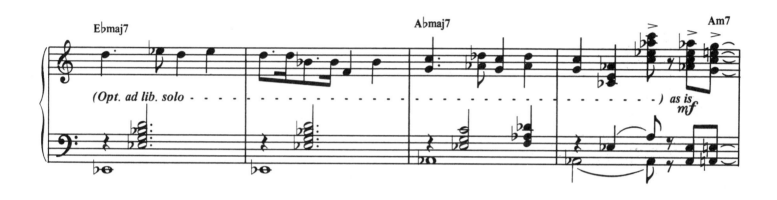

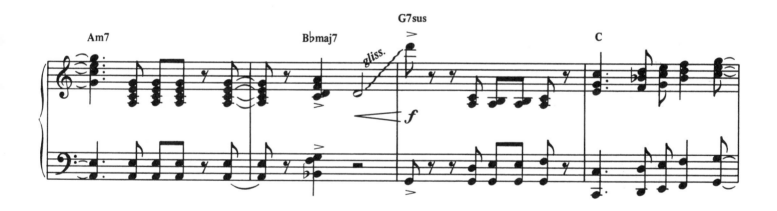

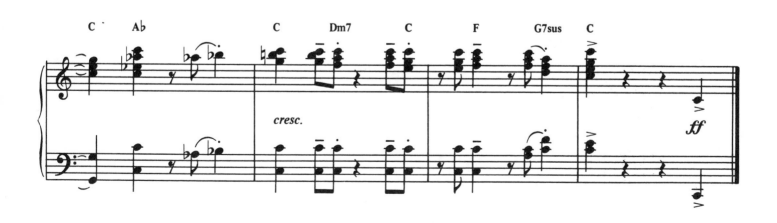

Rocky & Bullwinkle

from the Cartoon Television Series

By FRANK COMSTOCK

94

Simon and Simon
from the Television Series

By BARRY DeVORZON
and MICHAEL TOWERS

Moderately

© Copyright 1982, 1984 by MCA - ON BACKSTREET MUSIC, INC. and MCA - DUCHESS MUSIC CORPORATION
International Copyright Secured   All Rights Reserved
MCA Music Publishing

Theme from "STAR TREK®"

from the Paramount Television Series STAR TREK ®

Words by GENE RODDENBERRY
Music by ALEXANDER COURAGE

(Roll Along) Wagon Train

from WAGON TRAIN

Words by JACK BROOKS
Music by SAMMY FAIN

This Is It
Theme from THE BUGS BUNNY SHOW

Words and Music by MACK DAVID
and JERRY LIVINGSTON

Wings
Theme from the Paramount Television Series WINGS

"Sonata In A" by FRANZ SCHUBERT
as Adapted and Arranged by ANTONY COOKE

With a Little Help from My Friends

featured in THE WONDER YEARS

Words and Music by JOHN LENNON
and PAUL McCARTNEY

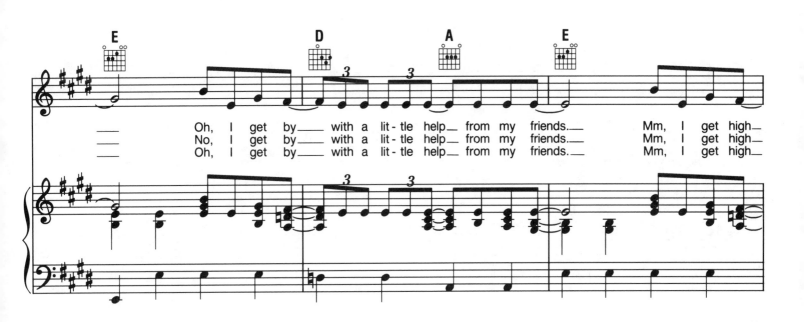

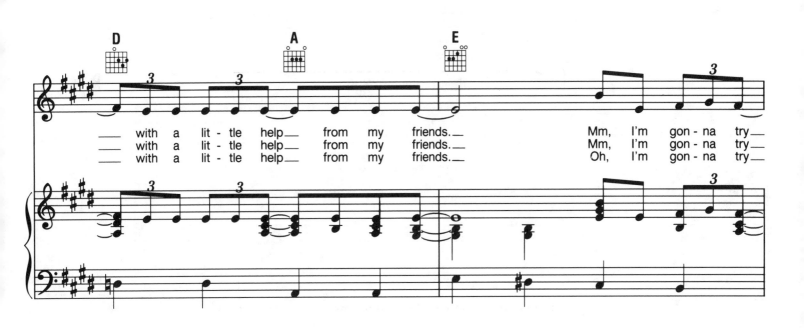

111

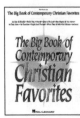